THE TIME MACHINE

by
H. G. Wells

Teacher Guide

Written by
Pat Watson

Note

The 2002 Modern Library paperback edition of the book, © 1895, 1923 by H.G. Wells, © 1931 by Random House, Inc., was used to prepare this guide. The page references may differ in other editions. Novel ISBN: 0-375-76118-7

Please note: Please assess the appropriateness of this book for the age level and maturity of your students prior to reading and discussing it with them.

ISBN 1-58130-525-7
Copyright infringement is a violation of Federal Law.

© 2004 by Novel Units, Inc., Bulverde, Texas. All rights reserved. No part of this publication may be reproduced, translated, stored in a retrieval system, or transmitted in any way or by any means (electronic, mechanical, photocopying, recording, or otherwise) without prior written permission from Novel Units, Inc.

Photocopying of student worksheets by a classroom teacher at a non-profit school who has purchased this publication for his/her own class is permissible. Reproduction of any part of this publication for an entire school or for a school system, by for-profit institutions and tutoring centers, or for commercial sale is strictly prohibited.

Novel Units is a registered trademark of Novel Units, Inc. Printed in the United States of America.

To order, contact your local school supply store, or—
Novel Units, Inc.
P.O. Box 97
Bulverde, TX 78163-0097

Web site: www.educyberstor.com

Lori Mammen, Editorial Director
Andrea M. Harris, Production Manager/Production Specialist
Kim Kraft, Product Development Manager/Curriculum Specialist
Suzanne K. Mammen, Curriculum Specialist
Heather Johnson, Product Development Specialist
Jill Reed, Product Development Specialist
Nancy Smith, Product Development Specialist
Pramilla Freitas, Production Specialist
Adrienne Speer, Production Specialist

Table of Contents

Summary 3

Characters 3

About the Author 4

Background Information 4

Initiating Activities 5

Eleven Sections 12
    Each section contains: Summary, Vocabulary,
    Discussion Questions, and Supplementary Activities

Post-reading Discussion Questions 26

Post-reading Extension Activities 28

Assessment 29

Scoring Rubric 30

Glossary 31

Skills and Strategies

Thinking
Analysis, compare/contrast, research, critical thinking

Vocabulary
Target words, definitions

Literary Elements
Characterization, simile, metaphor, allusion, personification, plot development, setting, theme, foreshadowing, irony, genre

Writing
Poetry, essay, eulogy, script, sequel, newspaper articles and headlines

Listening/Speaking
Discussion, dramatization, music

Comprehension
Cause/effect, prediction

Across the Curriculum
Art—sketch, collage, montage; Music—ballad; Current Events—newspaper and magazine articles

Genre: science fiction

Setting: England, late 1890s; the future, 802,701

Point of View: primarily first-person narrative; some areas spoken by the Time Traveller

Themes: fear, adventure, survival, friendship, resourcefulness, human nature

Subjects: invention, man's limitations, scientific possibilities, social and cultural evolution/devolution of man

Conflict: person vs. evil, person vs. nature, person vs. self

Style: narrative

Tone: pessimistic (human evolution, the future), contemplative

Date of First Publication: 1895

Summary

The innovative, brave Time Traveller hurtles into the future after boarding his Time Machine. He arrives in the year 802,701 and encounters what appears to be a utopian society of advanced human beings. As he explores the future world, however, he begins to uncover a dark secret that is leading mankind to its inevitable doom. During his struggle to survive and escape back to his own time era, he discovers a decaying society and an unusual force of evil. In his futuristic adventure, he finds and loses a gentle friend, experiences unbelievable fear, and utilizes his own ingenuity. He faces his skeptical friends when he returns to the present. He then leaves again.

Characters

The Time Traveller: inventive, confident, courageous protagonist; relates his tale of the future in a first-person narrative; struggles and survives against evil in a future world

narrator: unnamed intellectual; explains the Time Traveller's pre- and post-travel discussions with his friends

Filby: red-headed, argumentative; the only person other than the Time Traveller referred to by name

Psychologist: rational, inquisitive; thinks the Time Traveller tricks them with his model of the Time Machine

Very Young Man: excited about the prospect of traveling in time

Provincial Mayor: mayor of the province

Medical Man: interested; eventually believes the Time Traveller suffers from overwork

Blank, the Editor: interested in facts; believes the Time Traveller's story is false

Dash, the Journalist: wants a factual account

Chose, the Silent Man: shy, quiet; says nothing

Weena: gentle, naïve, exquisite; Traveller's friend in the future world

About the Author

Personal: Herbert George Wells was born in 1866, in Bromley, Kentucky. He spent three years as an apprentice to a draper in Windsor and Southsea. In 1883, he received a scholarship to further his education at the Royal College of Science, where he studied under biologist T. H. Huxley. His interest in biology later influenced his writing of science fiction. Following a short teaching career, he became a full-time writer in 1893. He married his cousin Isabel in 1891 but left her to marry one of his students, Amy Catherine Robbins, in 1895. They had two sons. A liaison with Amber Reeves produced a daughter, and a ten-year relationship with a young English author, Rebecca West, produced a son. Wells died in 1946.

Literary Career: Wells became well-known with the publication of *The Time Machine*, his first major fiction work. He followed it with *The Island of Dr. Moreau* (1896), *The Invisible Man* (1897), and *The War of the Worlds* (1898). Later fiction works include *Love and Mr. Lewisham* (1900) and *The New Machiavelli* (1911). He also published several non-fiction works, including *The Outline of History* (1920), *The Science of Life* (1929–1930), and *Experiment in Autobiography* (1934). Wells continued to write prolifically, producing his last work, *Mind at the End of Its Tether*, in 1945. In addition to his literary pursuits, he joined the socialist Fabian Society in 1903. He was a member of the Research Committee of the League of Nations and published several books about the world organization. He was a Labour candidate for Parliament. Additional information can be accessed: http://www.kirjasto.sci.fi/hgwells.htm. (Web site was active at the printing of this guide.)

Background Information

1. The Fabian Society is a group of British socialists that was founded in 1884. Fabians teach that socialism can be achieved gradually through a series of reforms. The Fabians differ from communists, who believe that the people can gain ownership of the means of production only through revolution. The society's ideas became the basis of the British Labor Party. H. G. Wells was a noted Fabian.

2. Sphinx: In Greek mythology, the Sphinx proposed a riddle to every passerby and killed those unable to guess it. The Time Traveller observes the White Sphinx soon after arriving in the future.

3. The movie: 1960; starring Rod Taylor; 103 minutes. Note the differences: (a) Before the Time Traveller, now named George, reaches 802,701, he sees the effects of World Wars I and II and an atomic attack on England. The Eloi are the descendants of people who remained on the surface during the nuclear attack, and the Morlocks are the descendants of people who survived in bomb shelters. (b) The Traveller and Weena fall in love. (c) The movie ends with the Traveller starting on a quest to rescue Weena. Consider viewing the movie as a culmination to reading the novel. Compare/contrast the plot. Note that the book reflects 1895 concerns such as social status, e.g., the aristocracy and the working class, and fears about the financial system. The movie reflects concerns of the 1960s, e.g., fear of nuclear war, concerns about communism.

4. The following prereading vocabulary will enhance students' understanding of the book: (a) socialism: system of social organization that seeks government ownership or regulation of the principal means of production; followers believe in peaceful, legal methods to achieve their goals (b) communism: political and economic system in which the government owns the land, factories, and other economic resources; followers believe in using force to achieve goals (c) capitalism: economic structure that emphasizes control of

the economy by individual households and privately owned businesses (d) utopia: an ideal society with justice and equality for all citizens (e) dystopia: opposite of utopia; a place that is bad or imperfect (f) evolution: process of positive change over a long period of time; regeneration (g) devolution: reversed evolution; degeneration (h) optimism: tendency to look on the bright side of things; belief that everything will turn out for the best and good will finally prevail over evil (i) pessimism: tendency to look on the dark side of things; belief that there is more evil than good

Initiating Activities

1. Place the phrase "science fiction" on an overhead transparency. Brainstorm with students concerning their interpretation of the phrase, books they have read, and movies they have seen. Emphasize that a literary work of science fiction combines science with fantasy and deals with life in the future, in other galaxies, or in other fantasy situations.

2. Place the phrase "The Time Machine" on an overhead transparency. Elicit students' responses: those who have heard of or read the book, those who have seen the movie, possible connotations of the phrase, and possible content of the book.

3. On their own paper, have students draw a time line divided into 100-year segments, placing the current year in the middle. Have them list past events they would like to visit and events they project into the future.

4. Have students keep a journal of questions to ask in class as they read.

5. Read aloud the "teasers" on the back cover, then preview the book. Brainstorm with students about the title, the author, the cover and other illustrations, when the book was written, and why the chapters are not titled.

6. Students should keep a list of foreshadowing in the novel as they read (see Foreshadowing Chart on page 7 of this guide).

Prediction Chart

What characters have we met so far?	What is the conflict in the story?	What are your predictions?	Why did you make these predictions?

Foreshadowing Chart

Foreshadowing is the literary technique of giving clues to coming events in a story.

Directions: List at least four examples of foreshadowing you notice as you read the novel. Explain what clues are given, then list the coming event that is suggested.

Foreshadowing	Page #	Clues	Coming Event

Character Web

Directions: Complete the attribute web by filling in information specific to a character in the book.

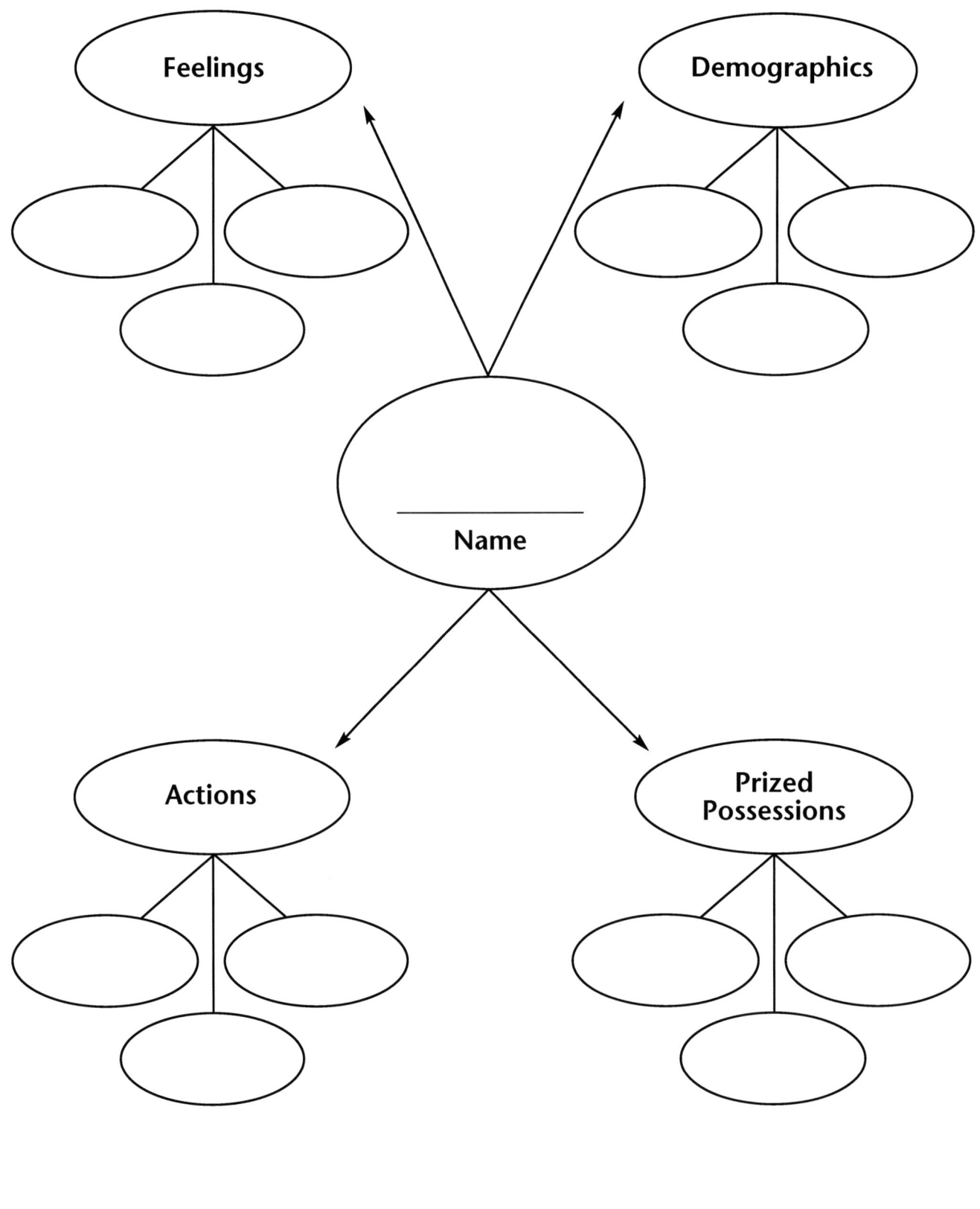

Fishbone Map

Directions: List the effect (or result) in the box. Consider the causes. List cause 1, 2, 3, 4 (as appropriate). Add details to support the causes you list.

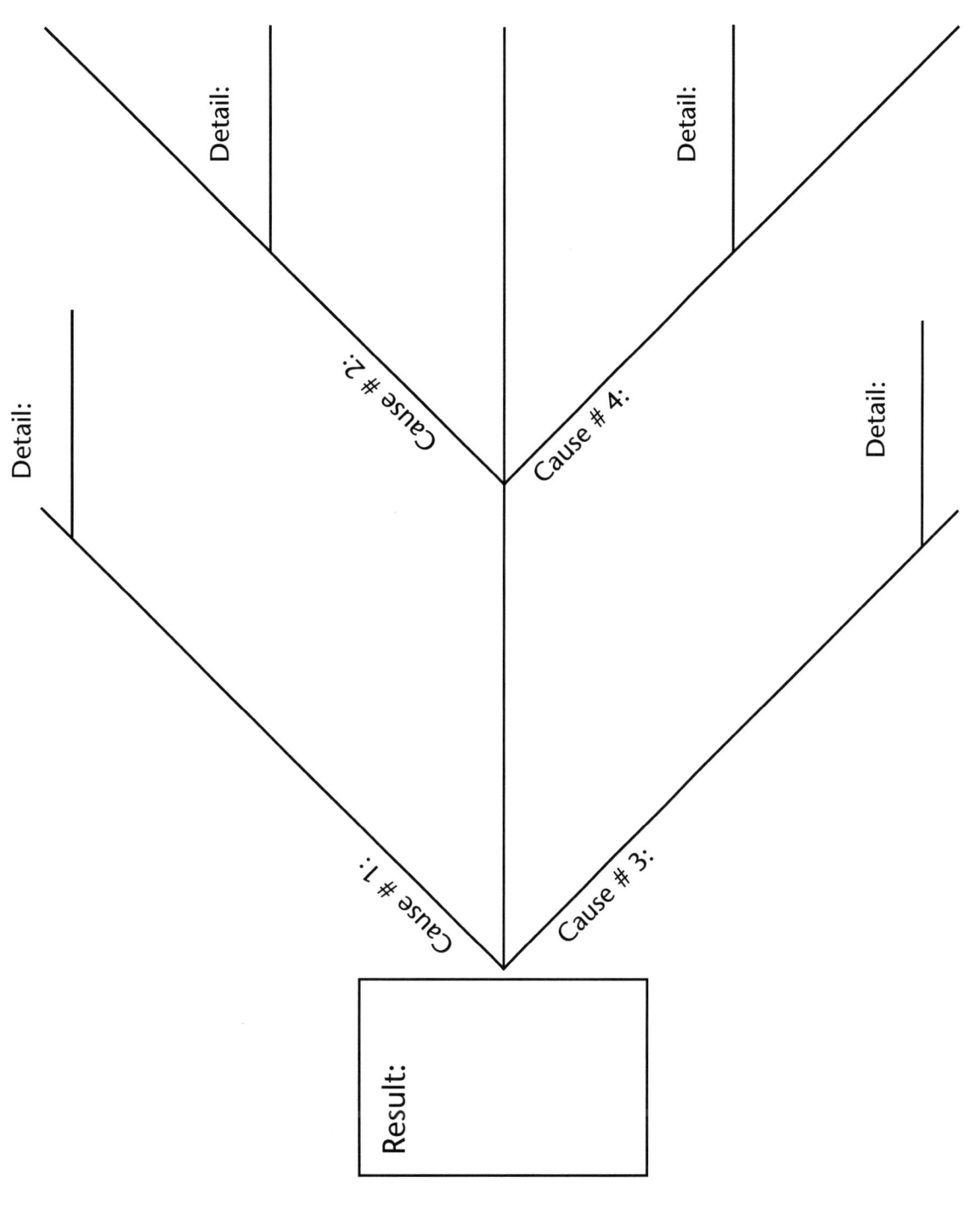

Story Map

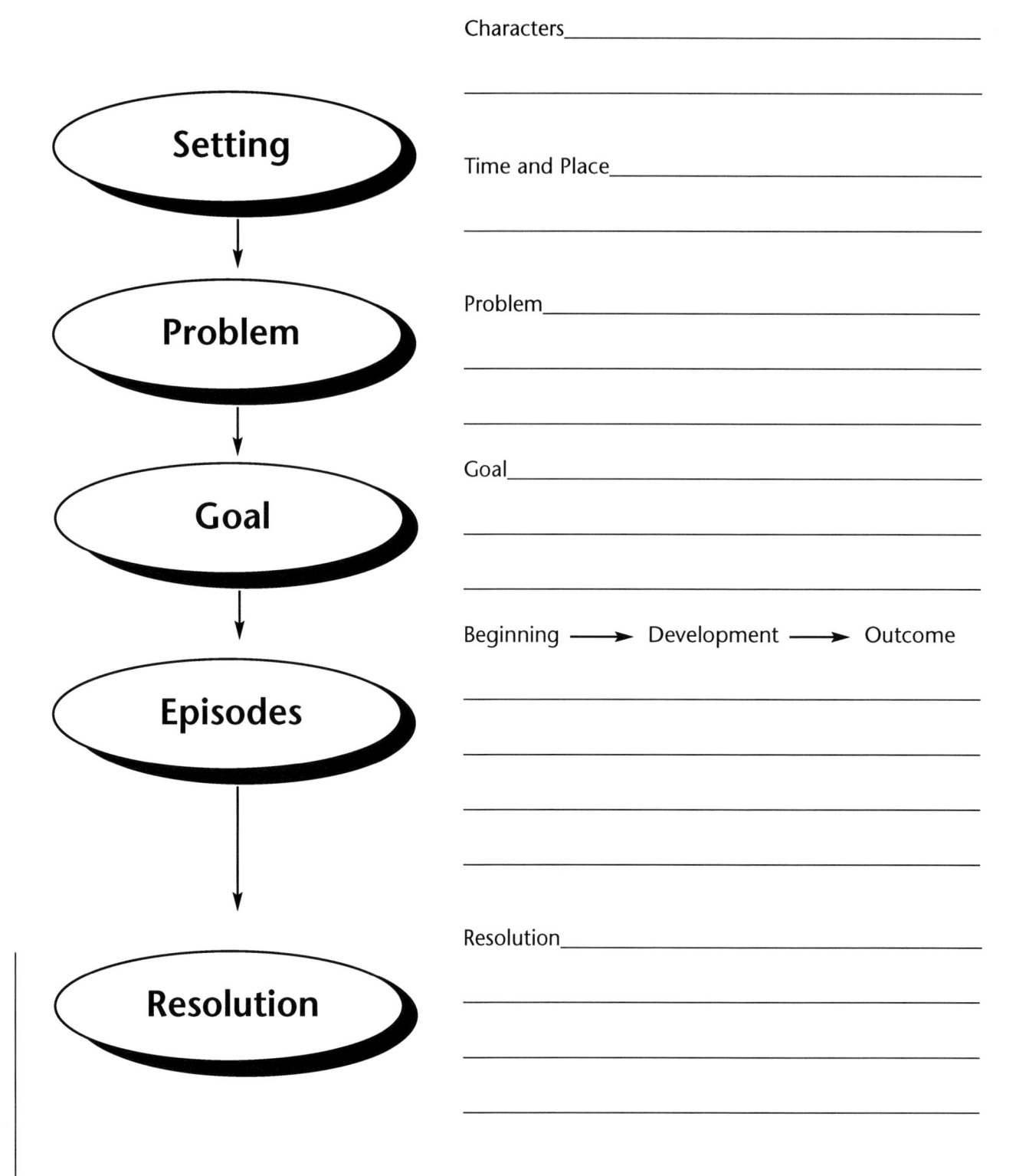

Characters _____

_____

Time and Place _____

_____

Problem _____

_____

_____

Goal _____

_____

Beginning ⟶ Development ⟶ Outcome

_____

_____

_____

_____

Resolution _____

_____

_____

- Setting
- Problem
- Goal
- Episodes
- Resolution

Thematic Analysis

Directions: Choose a theme from the book to be the focus of your word web. Complete the web and then answer the question in each starred box.

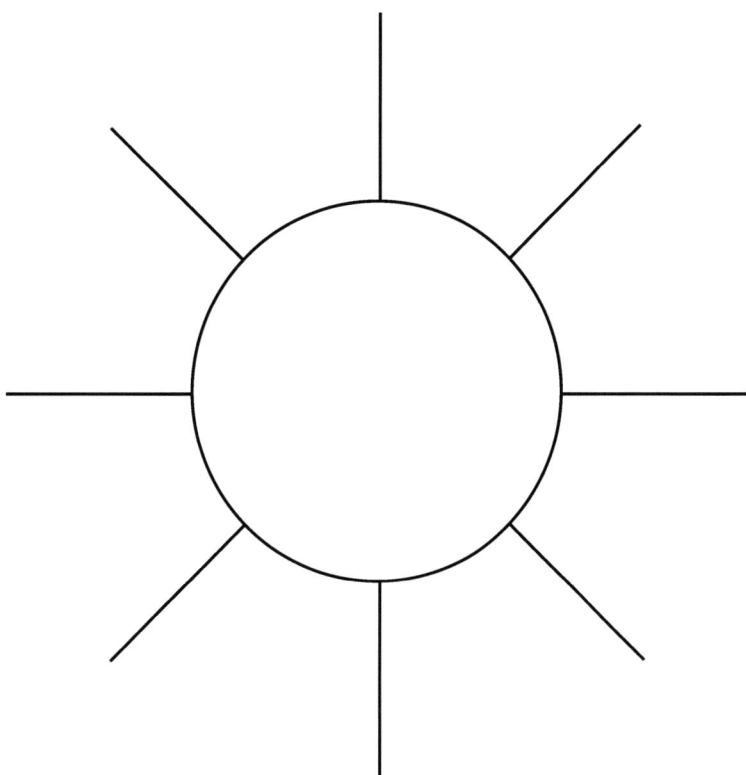

What is the author's main message?	What did you learn from the book?

Note: Where applicable, examples of literary devices found in each section are included in the Supplementary Activities. Guide students to identify these devices as they read the novel. Some sections include an Enrichment Activity (identified by *) for accelerated students.

Chapter 1, pp. 3–11

The Time Traveller tells his friends about his Time Machine. He demonstrates a model of his mechanism, then shows them the actual machine and announces his intention to explore time. They believe he has tricked them.

Vocabulary
recondite (3)
paradox (4)
fecundity (4)
introspective (5)
communistic (8)
plausible (11)

Discussion Questions

1. Examine what the first chapter reveals about the Time Traveller and his latest invention. *(He is an intelligent inventor who is excited about his latest experiment, on which he has worked for two years. He demonstrates his scientific knowledge as he explains his theory of the geometry of Four Dimensions, i.e., Time is the fourth dimension of space, and counters their skepticism with rational logic. As he expounds his idea for time travel to his friends, he reveals that he has invented a machine that will travel through time, past or future. He shows them a model of his Time Machine and explains how it works. The Psychologist triggers the lever that sends the machine into time. The Time Traveller then shows them the big machine and announces his intention to explore time. pp. 3–11)*

2. Discuss information about the Traveller's friends. Analyze the significance of their titles and how each guest symbolizes an aspect of humanity. Why is Filby the only one who has a specific name? *(Filby is argumentative and questions every idea the Traveller presents. The Psychologist is skeptical, wants a rational explanation, and doesn't believe the Traveller is logical. He doesn't want the others to think he is disturbed by things he can't explain. The Provincial Mayor fits his name, i.e., he is the mayor of a province but he is also provincial [unsophisticated] in that he doesn't think "outside the box" and is slow to grasp a new idea. The Very Young Man exhibits youthful enthusiasm and willingness to accept new ideas. The Medical Doctor is open to new ideas but wants proof. Each of the titles represents the personality traits of the individual. The titles symbolize the skeptic, the person with limited thinking and lack of vision, the enthusiasm of youth, and the person who insists on proof before accepting anything new. Answers will vary. pp. 4–11)*

3. Analyze the Time Traveller's explanation of the geometry of Four Dimensions. Note the discussion about moving freely up and down. Discuss recent inventions that allow people to move up and down. *(He believes that, in addition to the recognized space dimensions of Length, Breadth, and Thickness, Time is a fourth dimension in which people can move about. In his opinion, Time can be measured and observed just as clearly as the Length, Breadth, and Thickness of space. The Medical Man mentions the ability to move up and down in balloons. Possible answers: various types of aircraft, bungee jumping, pogo sticks, etc. pp. 5–6)*

4. Discuss the significance of the narrator's statement, "To discover a society erected on a strictly communistic basis" (p. 8). Discuss prior knowledge of or speculation about communism. *(He envisions a future society that will be totally communistic, i.e., a political and economic system in which the government owns the land, factories, and other economic resources. This reflects Wells' philosophy as a member of the socialistic Fabian Society, which teaches basically the same concepts as communism but believes its goals can be achieved gradually through a series of reforms.)*

5. Examine the Time Traveller's explanation of the model of his Time Machine and analyze the reactions of his friends. *(The mechanism is relatively simple, with a lever to push forward for the future or backward for the past, and a saddle seat for the traveler. The Traveller explains the mechanism carefully and assures the others that no trickery is involved. He is willing to waste the model to prove his point. The others are on the alert, expecting a trick. After the model disappears, the narrator is sure there is no trickery, and the others react with a mixture of belief and doubt. The Traveller is nonchalant. pp. 8–11)*

6. Analyze the implication of the Medical Man's question, "Or is this a trick...?" and of Filby's wink (p. 11). *(The Time Traveller has tricked them before. This explains, in part, why most of his friends are skeptical and wary. Filby does not believe the Traveller even when he vows he is telling the truth.)*

7. Find an example of personification on page 3 of the novel. *(The chairs embraced and caressed those who sat upon them.)*

8. **Prediction:** Will the Time Traveller actually be able to travel into the future? If so, what will he find?

Supplementary Activities

1. Drama: Working in small groups, stage the scene involving the departure of the Time Machine model.
2. *Research/Writing: Work with a partner and research the allusions on page 7 of the novel: the Battle of Hastings, Homer, and Plato. Choose one allusion and write a brief explanation of its importance to history.
3. Comprehension: Begin the Prediction Chart on page 6 of this guide using what you know from reading Chapter 1.
4. Art: Design your impression of the Time Machine.

Chapter 2, pp. 12–17

Some new characters are introduced. The Time Traveller arrives late for a dinner with his friends. He is disheveled, tired, and hungry. He tells them he has been time traveling. He agrees to tell his story but wants to do so without interruption.

Vocabulary
ingenuity (12)
anachronism (12)
jocular (13)
cadger (14)
caricature (15)
verbatim (16)
intonation (17)

Discussion Questions

1. Analyze the simile, "trusting their reputations for judgment with him was like furnishing a nursery with egg-shell china" (p. 12). *(Although his friends acknowledge the Time Traveller's ingenuity, none of them really believes in the Time Machine. They suspect that he plans to play a joke on them. People who do take him seriously risk their reputations if and when he reveals his trickery. The Traveller has the ability to destroy their reputations just as children playing in a nursery can cause fragile china to crash around them.)*

2. Examine the narrator's next meeting with the Time Traveller. Note the new characters and the absence of previous characters. Why does the author eliminate Filby, the Mayor, and the Very Young Man? *(The narrator and other guests arrive for a scheduled meeting with the Traveller one week after their prior meeting. The Doctor [Medical Man] has received a note explaining that the Traveller may be late and will explain when he comes. During dinner, the narrator half-jokingly suggests that the Traveller may be time traveling. The Editor asks for an explanation. The Psychologist is giving his account of the "ingenious paradox and trick" when the Traveller appears. Previous guests: the narrator, the Doctor, the Psychologist; new guests: the Editor [Blank], the Journalist [Dash], and the Silent Man [Chose]. Answers will vary. Suggestions: The Editor and Journalist are present to give a factual account of the Traveller's journey; Filby is eliminated because of his argumentative nature, the Mayor because of his reluctance to accept anything new, and the Very Young Man is replaced by a quiet, shy man who listens without comment. pp. 13–16)*

3. Analyze how the author builds suspense in this chapter. *(The Traveller arrives late, the others discuss the possibility that he has traveled in time, he arrives disheveled and haggard, he has no shoes, his socks are bloody, he is hungry, and he alludes to living for eight days as no human has ever lived. pp. 12–17)*

4. Analyze what the Editor means by his allusion to the Time Traveller's "Nebuchadnezzar phases" (p. 15). Note the Time Traveller's appearance. *(Nebuchadnezzar was a Babylonian king whose pride caused him to be reduced to living with the beasts of the fields for seven years, eating grass like an ox. The Time Traveller arrives disheveled, dusty, dirty, and smeared with green. His face is ghastly pale, his expression is haggard and drawn, and he is limping, wearing only bloody socks. He is hungry for meat. King Nebuchadnezzar went from one extreme to the other because of his pride. After proudly proclaiming one week prior that time travel is possible, he now returns showing signs of going from one extreme to another, e.g., pride to embarrassment.)*

5. Discuss the reaction of the Editor and the Journalist to the Time Traveller's arrival and examine what this reveals about the two men. Correlate with news stories today, e.g., some are strictly factual, others are sensational such as tabloid stories. *(Both men want the facts and begin mentally to develop a news story. The Editor immediately tries to question the Time Traveller and refers to a headline about the "Remarkable Behavior of an Eminent Scientist." He probes the other men with questions. Both the Journalist and the Editor will not believe the account of time travel and treat the story irreverently. When the Time Traveller reappears, the Editor demands a story and offers to pay for a word-for-word account although he still insists the story is false. Both men are skeptical but are primarily interested in a news story. pp. 14–16)*

6. Examine the Time Traveller's reaction to the guests. *(He refuses to discuss anything until he has something to eat. He acknowledges that he has been time traveling and, after eating, begins his tale. He agrees to tell of his adventure but refuses to argue and demands that his guests refrain from interrupting him. He begins a story that enthralls his guests. pp. 16–17)*

7. **Prediction:** What tale will the Time Traveller unfold?

Supplementary Activities

1. Writing: Write headlines for a factual or sensational news story about the Time Traveller. Share with the class and discuss the type of story each headline would indicate.

2. *Creative Writing: The Time Traveller's guests are skeptical about his story. Write a metaphor or simile poem about "skepticism." Pattern—Line 1: noun; Lines 2–4: write something about the subject, with each line saying something different and giving an idea of what the subject is like; Line 5: a metaphor or simile that begins with the title

Chapter 3, pp. 17–22

The Time Traveller tells of his departure aboard the Time Machine and his arrival in the future. He lands in a hailstorm, sees a colossal white sphinx and other vast shapes, and men running. One slight, frail creature approaches him.

Vocabulary
velocity (18)
luminous (18)
rudimentary (19)
sphinx (21)
verdigris (21)
temerity (21)
consumptive (22)

Discussion Questions

1. Analyze the Time Traveller's statement, "I suppose a suicide who holds a pistol to his skull feels much the same wonder at what will come next as I felt then" (p. 17). *(He is the first to attempt travel into time and has no idea what will happen to him, just as a person who holds a pistol to his head does not know what awaits him if he goes through with his plan. The Time Traveller is apprehensive, yet determined to explore the unknown.)*

2. Discuss the sensations the Time Traveller experiences as he launches into the future. Note the similes that describe his travels. *(The clock moves rapidly, and the laboratory becomes increasingly faint and hazy. He experiences unpleasant sensations such as a helpless headlong motion and the fear of an impending crash. Night follows day rapidly, and he sees the sun and moon moving swiftly across the sky. He moves too quickly to be aware of moving things, traveling over a year a minute. The unpleasant sensations merge into frantic exhilaration. Similes: Mrs. Watchett seems to shoot across the room like a rocket. He sees trees growing and changing like puffs of vapour, huge buildings rise and pass like dreams, and architecture that seems to be built of glimmer and mist. pp. 17–19)*

3. Examine the Time Traveller's reluctance to stop the Time Machine and his ultimate decision. *(Because he is traveling at such high velocity, he is afraid coming to a stop will cause him, molecule by molecule, to be jammed into whatever lies in his way. This may create an explosion that will blow himself and his machine into the unknown, out of all possible dimensions. He thinks he can never stop, then resolves to stop immediately. He flies headlong through the air and lands safely. pp. 19–20)*

4. Discuss what the Time Traveller sees when he lands and analyze his feelings of being naked in a strange world. Note the simile, "I felt as perhaps a bird may feel in the clear air, knowing the hawk wings above and will swoop" (p. 21). *(He lands in a hailstorm on a green lawn surrounded by various flowers. He sees a huge, weather-worn white marble figure shaped like a winged sphinx that gives him the impression of disease. He observes other large buildings and a group of robed figures. One, a slight, frail creature, approaches him. At first he is terrified and feels naked, with no place to hide and nothing with which to defend himself, i.e., like a bird with no defense against a swooping hawk. pp. 20–22)*

5. Analyze the symbolism of the White Sphinx. *(The sphinx is the focal point of the countryside. It is weather-worn and imparts the suggestion of disease. The Traveller feels its sightless eyes "watching" him and the lips faintly smiling at him. The sphinx symbolizes the inhuman, unsympathetic, overwhelmingly powerful evil the Traveller fears and which he will ultimately find in the Morlocks. Just as he cannot escape the "eyes" of the sphinx, the Eloi cannot escape the Morlocks. The future is filled with the "disease" of apathy and complacency. p. 21)*

6. **Prediction:** What experiences will the Time Traveller encounter in the future world?

Supplementary Activities
1. Research/Art: As a class, research information about the sphinx. Draw your impression of the White Sphinx the Time Traveller sees when he lands in the future or bring pictures of sphinxes to class.
2. Literary Devices: Find and list a simile and metaphor from this section. This will be an ongoing assignment throughout the book. **Similes**—"night followed day like the flapping of a black wing" (p. 18); "hail…drove along the ground like smoke" (p. 20); "downpour… vanished like the trailing garments of a ghost" (p. 21) **Metaphors**—sun: streak of fire (p. 18); hail: curtain (p. 21)

Chapter 4, pp. 22–32
The Time Traveller arrives in the year A.D. 802,701 and discovers that the future creatures all look alike and live together in one large, dilapidated hall. They eat nothing but fruit. They show little interest in anything, and the Traveller realizes he has happened upon declining humanity.

Vocabulary
hypertrophied (25)
indolent (26)
precipitous (27)
intimation (27)
precocious (28)
griffins (29)
ameliorating (29)
subjugation (30)
connubial (31)

Discussion Questions
1. Discuss the Time Traveller's initial contact with the future men. Note his reactions to and interactions with them. *(They are gentle, graceful, and childlike. They are curious about the stranger and show no fear but do not attempt to communicate with him. All of them look and act alike and childishly interact with each other and with the Traveller, viewing him as a plaything. They take him to a large, dilapidated hall, and he realizes they all live together there. The creatures eat nothing but fruit. The Traveller feels out of place because of his size and his clothes. He attempts to communicate with them by learning their speech, but the creatures soon lose interest in him. pp. 22–27)*

2. Analyze the Traveller's interpretation of his discoveries about the futuristic men, their lifestyle, and their world. *(The ruinous, decaying structures he finds indicate to him the decline of civilization. He realizes he has entered a world of uniformity with communal living and people who are exactly alike. Although the people apparently live in ease and security, they have become complacent, apathetic, and frail because they no longer have any social or economic struggles. Their decline physically and mentally is evident in their slight stature, their lack of intelligence, and their indifference. He foresees that even the small amount of artistic impetus, e.g., singing, dancing, they have left will fade into inactivity. pp. 27–32)*

3. Compare what evolutionary changes the Traveller expects to find and what he does find. *(He expects to find stronger, more intelligent people who have developed a more organized world. He finds what he presumes to be people who have eliminated disease and troublesome insects and weeds. They are beautifully clothed and apparently happy, yet they have lost all individuality. pp. 29–31)*

4. Examine the Traveller's statement, "The ruddy sunset set me thinking of the sunset of mankind" (p. 29). Discuss whether Wells expresses pessimism or optimism about the future of mankind. *(The sun sets in a flash of glowing beauty, then fades into night. The Time Traveller sees mankind clothed beautifully and living carefree lives, yet he believes they are fading away. Answers will vary.)*

5. Analyze the Traveller's summation of hardship and freedom and the aftermath when struggles cease. *(Although he initially concludes that he has arrived in a utopia, i.e., social paradise, he begins to see that hardship and freedom are conditions which promote self-restraint, patience, and decision-making skills. Adversity causes the stronger people to survive and the weaker to decline, yet reaching the point where adversity is eliminated causes people to grow physically and mentally weak. When they cease to care about anything but their own pleasure, society will die. pp. 31–32)*

6. **Prediction:** What will the Time Traveller discover is wrong with his theory about the future world?

Supplementary Activities

1. Writing/Art: Complete the statement, "Apathy is…" or sketch your impression of the future people.

2. Literary Devices: **Similes**—"I could fancy myself flinging the whole dozen of them about like nine pins" (p. 23); "river lay like a band of burnished steel" (p. 29); see also pp. 23, 26, 28
Metaphors—Time Traveller: plaything (p. 24); earth: garden (p. 29)

Chapter 5, pp. 32–48

The Time Traveller reacts angrily and aggressively when he cannot find his Time Machine. He discovers many wells with the sounds of engines coming from them. Weena becomes his constant companion after he rescues her from drowning. He encounters a strange nocturnal creature who lives underground. He identifies the two species as Eloi (Upper-world) and Morlocks (Underworld).

Vocabulary

inarticulate (34)
stolid (36)
repugnance (36)
monomania (37)
subterranean (38)
decadent (39)
interpolated (40)
expostulations (41)
lemur (44)
nocturnal (45)
ramifications (46)

Discussion Questions

1. Analyze the introduction of conflict into the plot and how the Time Traveller reacts. *(He discovers his Time Machine is missing and faces the possibility of forever being stranded in the future. Fear consumes him, and he frantically searches for the machine but finds no trace of it. He rebukes himself for leaving it, but consoles himself with having the forethought to remove the levers by which it operates. He believes he has misjudged the intelligence of the people. He runs frenziedly about, sobbing and raving. When he comes to another building where people are sleeping, he angrily demands to know where his machine is. Realizing how frightened the people are, he runs out into the night and finally falls asleep on the ground. Losing his machine causes the Traveller to feel hopelessly cut off from his own people, but he reasons that he can eventually make another. He resolves to stay calm and patient, to find where they have hidden his machine, and to recover it by force or cunning. pp. 32–35)*

2. Discuss the Time Traveller's analysis of what has happened to his Time Machine and what he does. Analyze the irony of his situation and note the foreshadowing of future events. *(After examining the area around his landing spot, he discovers strange footprints in a groove in the grass. He finds panels on either side of the pedestal of the sphinx and concludes that his machine is inside the pedestal. He attempts to get two of the people to open it for him, but they react as if they are insulted. When he bangs on the panel with his fist, he hears something stir and chuckle inside. After realizing he cannot get inside the pedestal, he decides to be patient, to learn the ways of this future world, and find clues that will help him solve his problem. Finally, he laughs at his own entrapment. Irony: he has worked for years to get to the future and now wants to escape. Foreshadowing: the hint at the existence of other, evil creatures who will try to harm him. pp. 36–37)*

3. Examine information about the wells and towers and the Traveller's conclusion about them. *(He finds several circular wells, many of them very deep. He peers into the shaft of one but can see no sign of water. A sound like the thumping of a large engine comes from all the wells, and he discovers a steady downdraft of air in the shafts. He believes there is a connection between the wells and several tall towers on the slopes of land, concluding that they form an extensive system of subterranean ventilation. pp. 38–39)*

4. Examine issues that puzzle the Traveller about the future culture. *(He finds no signs of cremation or tombs, he has observed no one who is old or sick, and he finds no evidence of where the people get their clothes, e.g., no machinery, appliances, workshops, or stores. pp. 39–40)*

5. Discuss how the Traveller meets Weena and how they interact with each other. Analyze her fear and what this reveals about her culture. *(While watching some of the people bathing, he realizes that one of them is drowning, and no one is trying to help. He rescues her [Weena] and leaves after making sure she is okay. Later in the day, he meets her again, and she gives him a large garland of flowers. They are friendly and communicative, and she becomes his constant companion. She clings to him just like a child. From Weena, the Traveller learns that fear has not left this future world. She dreads anything having to do with darkness, and he recalls never finding one of the people outside or sleeping alone after dark. Everyone in this culture fears the dark. This fear is evident when he attempts to question two people about what is in the well shaft. Weena cries with fear when he tries to question her about the subterranean creatures. pp. 40–41, 45, 48)*

6. Examine the Traveller's discovery of another species in the future world and its effect on him. *(He initially thinks he sees ghosts and one white, ape-like creature. He observes white figures and once sees several of them carrying a dark body. On the fourth day, he finds and enters a narrow gallery, where he detects a pair of eyes watching him. He reaches out and touches something soft, then sees a small, white, ape-like figure with large grayish-red eyes and blond hair on its head and down its back. The creature vanishes down the well shaft. He concludes that man has evolved into two distinct animal species. He apprehensively wonders how the two species are related and what is hidden in the wells. pp. 42–45)*

7. Analyze the Traveller's suppositions about the new species he has discovered, the conclusions he draws about their relationship with the others, and how he classifies the two species. Analyze the types of division that exist today between the rich and the poor. *(He believes the second species to be subterranean, based on their bleached appearance, their large eyes, and their confusion in the sunshine. They live in underground tunnels that are ventilated by the towers pumping air through the well shafts. He concludes that these are the workers, producing materials underground for the comfort of those who live above ground. He classifies the two groups by the following terminology: (a) Capitalists, Haves, Upper-World people, aristocracy, beautiful race, frail creatures, Eloi; (b) Laborers, Have-Nots, Workers, Undergrounders, white things, ape-like creatures, Morlocks. Answers will vary. pp. 45–48)*

8. **Prediction:** What will happen to the Time Traveller if and when he encounters the Morlocks?

Supplementary Activities

1. Character Analysis/Creative Writing: List contrasting features of the Eloi and Morlocks, then write a cinquain poem about one of them. Pattern—Line 1: one word (noun), the title; Line 2: two words to describe the title; Line 3: three words to express action concerning the title; Line 4: four words to express feeling about the title; Line 5: one word that is a synonym for the title

2. Literary Devices: **Similes**—"I began, bawling like an angry child" (p. 34); the creature "was so like a human spider" (p. 44)

Chapter 6, pp. 48–53

The Time Traveller climbs down the well shaft and barely escapes from the Morlocks. His only defense is light, and they retreat when he lights matches.

Vocabulary
pallid (48)
façade (49)
disconcerted (50)
abysmal (51)
carnivorous (51)
lank (52)

Discussion Questions

1. Discuss the Time Traveller's conclusion about what he must do to recover his Time Machine and examine his reluctance to do so. Discuss a time when you had to do something courageous, whether or not you were alone, and how you felt. *(He believes he must go into the well and probe into the mysteries of the underground world. He is reluctant to do so because he feels so alone and defenseless. Answers will vary. pp. 48–49)*

2. Examine circumstances surrounding the Traveller's descent into the underground shaft and the effect his decision has on Weena. *(He procrastinates for two days by exploring more of the Upper-world territory but finally resolves to make his descent without wasting more time. Weena accompanies him and, when he begins his descent, she cries pitifully, runs to him, and attempts to pull him back. He becomes cramped and tired as he climbs about 200 yards down a shaft. He almost falls and is tempted to go back to the surface, but finally reaches the bottom. His eyes have difficulty adjusting to the darkness. pp. 49–50)*

3. Analyze what the Time Traveller discovers underground and why he is so frightened. Discuss the cause/effect of his exploration. *(The air is filled with the sound of machinery pumping air down the shaft. A soft hand touches his face, and he sees three creatures. They flee when he lights a match. He unsuccessfully attempts to converse with them. He feels his way down a tunnel to a large open space, lights another match, and sees a vast cavern with shapes like large machines. Morlocks lurk in the shadows. He smells fresh blood and sees the remains of a large animal the Morlocks had been eating. Cause: His match goes out. Effect: A hand touches him, and others begin to pick at his clothing. He becomes terribly frightened and shivers violently as they approach him more aggressively. Cause: He retreats to the narrow tunnel after lighting another match. Effect: Several hands clutch him when his light is blown out. Cause: He lights his final match. Effect: The Morlocks clutch his feet as his match goes out. He kicks at them and barely escapes. Cause: He quickly climbs up the shaft. Effect: The Morlocks peer up at him. Cause: Exhausted, he staggers into the sunlight. Effect: Weena kisses him; he hears other Eloi voices, then becomes insensible. pp. 51–53)*

4. Analyze the foreshadowing in this chapter. *(the Traveller's resolve to explore the Palace of Green Porcelain [p. 49]; Weena's irrational fear when the Traveller enters the shaft [p. 50]; scent of fresh blood and remnants of a carcass [p. 51]; the Traveller's lack of preparation for the journey [p. 52]; using up all his matches; his exhaustion and narrow escape from the Morlocks [p. 53])*

Supplementary Activities
1. Art: Sketch your impression of the Morlocks or bring to class pictures of various types of nocturnal creatures you think resemble the Morlocks.
2. Literary Devices: **Similes**—"shapes like big machines" (p. 51); "Morlocks rustling like wind among leaves, and pattering like the rain" (p. 53) **Metaphor**—match: wriggling red spot (p. 52)

Chapter 7, pp. 54–60

The Time Traveller determines to find a way to defend himself against the Morlocks. He and Weena begin their excursion to the Palace of Green Porcelain. He resolves to recover his Time Machine.

Vocabulary

malign (54)
hypothesis (54)
evolution (55)
Nemesis (55)
dexterous (56)
preternaturally (56)
vigil (58)
degradation (59)

Discussion Questions

1. Analyze the simile, "I felt like a beast in a trap, whose enemy would come upon him soon" (p. 54) and examine changes in the Time Traveller's attitude after his escape from the Morlocks. *(The discovery of the Morlocks makes him feel hopeless and despondent about his situation. He has believed himself capable of handling the childish Eloi, but the inhuman Morlocks make him feel like an animal in a trap waiting for his enemy to come, i.e., the darkness of the new moon. His fear is intensified by Weena's remarks about the dark nights, and he wonders what evil acts the Morlocks commit in the dark.)*

2. Discuss the Traveller's view of the evolution/devolution of the two species in the future world. Examine changes in the Eloi and the Morlocks and their co-dependency on each other. *(He believes the two species have developed a new relationship as the result of man's evolutionary decline. The previous relationship, with the Eloi as the aristocracy and the Morlocks as the working class, has passed away. Although the Eloi live above ground and the Morlocks live underground and make garments for the Eloi and help them maintain a semblance of their former lifestyle, the Morlocks do so for their own gain, i.e., they kill the Eloi in the darkness and eat them. The old social order is continuing to degenerate. The Eloi fear but need the Morlocks; the Morlocks know they are in control. pp. 54–55, 58–59)*

3. Examine the implications of the Traveller's excursion to the Palace of Green Porcelain. *(He determines to survive and knows he must have weapons and a place of refuge to do so. After finding nothing in the valley, he takes Weena and they start for the Palace, where he hopes to find refuge in the tall pinnacles, a means of fire for a torch with which to defend them, and a device to break open the doors and retrieve his Time Machine. Weena is delighted to go, and he carries her most of the way. As dark approaches, Weena becomes fearful, and the Traveller becomes weary and footsore. He wraps Weena in his jacket and keeps vigil beside her through the night. The Morlocks*

do not appear as long as he keeps vigil, implying that they are waiting for him to sleep. A loose heel on one shoe causes his ankle to swell. He throws the shoes away, implying that his travel will be slower and more difficult, making it harder to escape from the Morlocks. He plans to take Weena with him when he returns to his own time, implying his love for her. pp. 56–60)

4. Analyze the significance of the white flowers. *(Weena places them in his pocket on their journey to the Palace. As he tells his guests about his time travel, he places two withered flowers on the table. This adds credibility to his story. p. 56)*

5. **Prediction:** What will the Time Traveller find in the Palace of Green Porcelain?

Supplementary Activities

1. Creative Writing: List all the emotions you have observed in the Time Traveller since his arrival in the future, then choose one and write a metaphor or simile that describes that emotion.

2. Literary Devices: **Similes**—"They (the Morlocks) did it (work for Eloi) as a standing horse paws with his foot, or as a man enjoys killing animals in sport" (p. 55); "a faintness in the eastward sky, like the reflection of some colourless fire" (p. 58) **Metaphors**—jacket pocket: vase (p. 56); Milky Way: tattered streamer of star-dust (p. 58); Eloi: fatted cattle (p. 59) **Allusions**—Carlovingian kings: rulers of second Frankish dynasty; Charlemagne was a Carlovingian (p. 55); Faun: Roman mythological spirit, half-human, half-animal (p. 57); Carlyle: nineteenth-century social philosopher of Victorian England (p. 59)

Chapter 8, pp. 60–66

The Time Traveller and Weena arrive at the Palace of Green Porcelain, which he discovers is a decaying museum. He finds a club for defense, a usable box of matches, and camphor which he can use for a candle. He realizes the Morlocks are present.

Discussion Questions

Vocabulary

vestiges (60)
oblique (61)
deliquesced (62)
derelict (64)
hermetically (65)
volatile (65)

1. Discuss the Palace of Green Porcelain and analyze its symbolism. Which part of the decaying museum most disturbs the Time Traveller? *(It is deserted and falling into ruin. As the Traveller and Weena explore the building, he discovers that it is actually a museum. They find sections once devoted to paleontology, with remnants of dinosaur displays; mineralogy; natural history, with a few traces of stuffed animals; machines of all kinds; and chemistry, which is relatively well-preserved. They discover a library filled with decaying vestiges of books, a gallery of rusting firearms, an array of idols from many countries, and the model of a tin mine. The museum symbolizes the future loss of respect for the past, the decay of society, and the decline of humanity. Answers will vary. Suggestion: the library because he reflects on the enormous waste of labor in the thousands of pages of rotting paper and the fate of his own writing. pp. 60–66)*

2. Examine the weapons the Traveller finds and discuss which might prove to be the most effective. *(He breaks a club from one of the machines for a weapon and finds a box of usable matches and a sealed jar of camphor in the chemistry section. He can use the club to beat back approaching Morlocks, the matches to keep them at bay temporarily, and the camphor to create a longer lasting light. pp. 64–66)*

3. **Prediction:** What will the Time Traveller and Weena encounter on their return trip and will they reach their destination safely?

Supplementary Activities
1. Art: Working in small groups, create a montage of pictures representing the Palace of Green Porcelain or a sketch depicting the metaphor comparing the library to a sombre wilderness of rotting paper (p. 64).
2. Literary Devices: **Metaphor**—decaying books: wilderness of rotting paper (p. 64)

Chapters 9–10, pp. 66–75

Morlocks stalk the Time Traveller and Weena as they begin their trip back to the White Sphinx. He loses his way, lights the camphor, and falls asleep. He awakens to discover that the fire has gone out, his matches are missing, Weena is gone, and the Morlocks are surrounding him. The forest is on fire, and many Morlocks plunge into it. He returns to the White Sphinx, retrieves his Time Machine, and escapes.

Vocabulary

insidious (67)
carbuncles (69)
agape (70)
abominations (72)

Discussion Questions

1. Discuss the Time Traveller's plans and analyze the cause and effect of the mistakes he makes on the return trip. *(He begins the trip late in the day, planning to build a fire and sleep that night, then arrive at the White Sphinx early the next morning. Mistakes: he tries to carry firewood, which slows him down; he enters the wood when it is dark, knowing the Morlocks attack in the dark; he sets the firewood on fire, not realizing how quickly the dry forest will ignite; he turns around several times trying to maneuver Weena and the matches, causing him to lose his way; he falls into a deep sleep, allowing the fire to go out; he loses the matchbox, leaving him without his primary source of defense. pp. 66–71)*

2. Examine the reaction of the Morlocks to the forest fire. *(As the fire illuminates the sky, the Morlocks flee, and the Traveller follows them. Just as he steps into a clearing, a Morlock lunges past him and runs straight into the fire. The Morlocks are blinded and helpless by the fire. As they grope about in the heat, their confusion causes many of them to rush into the flames and perish. pp. 70–72)*

3. Analyze the Traveller's reaction to losing Weena. Analyze their relationship. Do you think she could possibly have survived? *(He searches diligently for her and realizes the Morlocks have left her in the forest. He is relieved to know she escaped the fate to which she seemed destined, i.e., her body being devoured by the Morlocks. He is deeply grieved by Weena's horrible death, and he once again feels terribly alone. In retrospect, he feels more the sorrow of a dream than of an actual loss. They have a loving friendship. She trusts him and wants to be with him constantly, showering him with pretty flowers and loving gestures. He protects her, carries her, and plans to take her back to the present with him. Answers will vary. p. 72, throughout)*

4. Analyze what the Traveller concludes about human intellect and how this correlates with intellectual versatility. *(He believes human intellect committed suicide because of its desire for comfort and ease and a balanced society of security and permanence. The rich became assured of wealth and comfort, and the worker became assured of his life and work, leaving no employment problems and no unsolved social questions. Intellectual versatility results when people experience*

change, danger, and trouble, and intelligence declines as the need for change ceases. The Upper-world people concentrated on being pretty, and the Underworld concentrated on mechanical industry. As the Upper-world became apathetic and complacent, they ceased to think and grow intellectually. They ceased to feed the laborers properly. The Under-world people had to continue to think in order to keep the machinery running. When they ran out of food, their thought processes led them to eat the people for whom they worked. pp. 73–74)

5. Analyze the comparison the Traveller makes between the Eloi and cattle. *(When he returns to the White Sphinx, everything looks the same, but he knows that the beauty of the Eloi covers the hidden world of darkness and their future fate. They spend their days pleasantly, eating and frolicking, just as cattle spend their days eating and growing fat. Both will be slaughtered for meat. p. 73)*

6. Discuss the Traveller's final confrontation with the Morlocks and the danger of his false assumption. *(When he approaches the White Sphinx to break the panel and retrieve his machine, he finds the valves open. He sees his machine inside, realizes the Morlocks will be waiting for him, but believes he knows their plan. As he examines the cleaned and oiled machine, the panels close, leaving him trapped in the dark as he expected. As the Morlocks come near him, he attempts to light a match but is unable to do so because he doesn't have the box on which he must strike it. He fights with them as he struggles to fit the levers onto the machine. He finally achieves his goal, pulls the lever, and escapes. His assumption about the matches almost costs him his life. pp. 74–75)*

Supplementary Activities

1. Drama: Working in small groups, stage one of the scenes in this section.
2. *Creative Writing: Write a eulogy for Weena.
3. Literary Devices: **Similes**—"the Morlocks' eyes shone like carbuncles" (p. 69); "I felt as if I was in a monstrous spider's web" (p. 70)

Chapter 11, pp. 76–80

The Time Traveller travels into the future and arrives at the end of the earth.

Vocabulary

prodigious (76)
sullen (77)
lurid (77)
apparition (78)
foliated (78)
undulating (79)

Discussion Questions

1. Examine the Traveller's departure, what he sees as he leaps into the future, and where he lands. *(He is not seated properly and has to cling to the machine for an indefinite time, not knowing where he is going. When he looks at the dials, he realizes he is traveling at an amazing velocity millions of years into the future. The rapid succession of day and night gradually settles into twilight over the earth. The sun grows broader and redder and no longer sets. The moon vanishes, and the stars become creeping points of light. The earth comes to rest facing the sun. He slowly reverses the motion of his machine, finally landing on a desolate beach in perpetual twilight. pp. 76–77)*

2. Analyze the Traveller's final experience in the future and its effect on him. *(The desolation around him causes him to shiver. Monstrous crabs surround him, and he retreats one month but*

can still see the crabs crawling around. An abominable despair, caused by the red eastern sky, the northward blackness, the Dead Sea, the monsters and poisonous plants, and the thin air, hangs over the world. He moves ahead 100 years, and things are the same except the sun is larger and duller. He travels ahead in increments of 1,000 years, slowly watching the earth die. He stops once more. The beach is flecked with white, and the temperature is bitterly cold. Only the Dead Sea is unfrozen under the eternal sunset. An eclipse begins, and darkness engulfs the silent world. The Traveller is sick and confused as he experiences the end of the earth. pp. 78–80)

3. Discuss the tone of this and preceding chapters. Discuss what Wells foresaw as the destiny of mankind and the earth as we know it. *(The tone is pessimistic. Answers will vary. Suggestion: He believed that, if mankind continued in the trend of social stratification and materialism, life as it then existed would cease. Man would destroy himself, and the earth would end. throughout)*

Supplementary Activities
1. Writing: Write the definitions for optimism and pessimism, then write a metaphor or simile about one of the perspectives.
2. *Creative Writing: Same as above for definitions; write a diamente poem contrasting the two perspectives. Pattern—Line 1: one word (a noun, the subject); Line 2: two words (adjectives describing line 1); Line 3: three words ("ing" or "ed" words that relate to line 1); Line 4: four words (first two nouns relate to line 1; second two nouns to line 7); Line 5: three words ("ing" or "ed" words that relate to line 7); Line 6: two words (adjectives describing line 7); Line 7: one word (noun that is the opposite of line 1)
3. Literary Devices: **Similes**—"a thing like a huge white butterfly"; "a crab as large as yonder table" (p. 78); "curved pale line like a vast new moon" (p. 79)

Chapter 12–Epilogue, pp. 81–86
The Time Traveller returns to the present and tells his story. Most of his friends think it is a lie, but the narrator goes to the Time Traveller's laboratory to verify the story. The Time Traveller leaves again and does not return.

Vocabulary
stagnant (82)
translucent (84)
truncated (85)
phantasm (85)
abysses (86)

Discussion Questions
1. Examine the Traveller's return to the present and his reaction to the events. *(He remains insensible for a long time during his return but gradually begins to breathe freely again. As the hands on the dials spin backward, he sees in reverse things he had seen on his journey into the future and finally returns to his laboratory. When he gets off the machine, he shakes and trembles. At first he thinks maybe he has dreamed it all but then notices that his machine is in a different location. He realizes that his friends may not believe him. pp. 81–82)*

2. Analyze the response of the Traveller's friends to his story of time travel and discuss the things that lend credibility to his story. *(The Doctor stares at him intently, the Editor stares at his cigar, the Journalist fumbles for his watch, and the others are motionless. The Editor thinks it is a pity he does not write stories, and the Doctor thinks he is overworked. They all go to see the Time*

Machine, but no one except the narrator believes the story could possibly be true and he wants more proof. Credibility: two white flowers; half-healed scars on his knuckles; spots, smears, grass, moss, and a bent handle on the machine. pp. 82–84)

3. Discuss the final communication between the Traveller and the narrator. *(The narrator returns to the laboratory because he wants to ask the Traveller some questions. The Traveller assures the narrator that the story is true and that he will prove it at lunch but must leave him temporarily. When the narrator goes to the laboratory door to tell the Traveller he must leave for an appointment, he hears odd sounds. He opens the door and discovers that the Traveller and his machine are gone. He realizes the Traveller has once again gone into the future to return with proof, i.e., specimens and photographs. After three years, the Traveller has not returned. pp. 84–85)*

4. Why doesn't the author reveal the Traveller's fate? *(Answers will vary. Suggestions: Wells might have intended to write a sequel [the story originally appeared as a serialization] or he wanted to leave the ending up to the reader's imagination.)*

5. Examine the content of the Epilogue and analyze what the narrator considers most important. *(The narrator speculates about what might have happened to the Traveller and whether or not he will ever return. He wonders if perhaps he traveled into the past and was captured by a creature or remains there in some other age. He thinks he may have traveled into a future where men have solved their problems. He reveals that the Traveller was pessimistic about the advancement of mankind. The narrator sees the future as black and blank, with occasional bright spots as he remembers the Traveller's story. The narrator believes it is most important that gratitude and tenderness still live in the hearts of men. The Epilogue reflects Wells' pessimistic view of the future of mankind. p. 86)*

Supplementary Activities

1. Writing: Choose an era from your time line (see Initiating Activities in this guide) and write a short narrative about something that happens to you during that time period.

2. Literary Devices: **Simile**—"mass swayed like a bough shaken by the wind" (p. 84)
Metaphor—life: a dream (p. 83)

Post-reading Discussion Questions

1. Using the Character Web on page 8 of this guide, characterize the Time Traveller or Weena. *(Traveller—Feelings: confident, frightened, dismayed, apprehensive; Demographics: resident of present time period, inventor, friend of many; Actions: builds Time Machine, travels into and returns from the future, tells his story; Prized Possessions: Time Machine, two white flowers. Weena—Feelings: naïve, loving, fearful; Demographics: resident of year A.D. 802,701, communal society, indistinguishable from others; Actions: plays, throws flowers, goes with Traveller; Prized Possessions: garlands of flowers.)*

2. Using the Fishbone Map on page 9 of this guide, examine the cause/effect of various incidents in the plot. *(Answers are addressed in Discussion Questions in this guide.)*

3. Using the Story Map on page 10 of this guide, discuss the plot development. *(Setting, characters, and episodes are found in this guide. Problem: the Time Traveller arrives in the future and struggles to return; conflict with the Morlocks; Goal: to discover another world; Resolution: he returns to the present but leaves again to bring back proof)*

4. Using the Thematic Analysis on page 11 of this guide, analyze one of the themes from the novel. *(Courage: the Traveller attempts to go where no one has ever gone before, i.e., forward in time; he goes into the well and encounters the Morlocks; he travels to the Palace of Green Porcelain; he battles the Morlocks on the return trip; he struggles valiantly to save Weena; he enters the White Sphinx to retrieve his machine; he travels to the end of the earth; he returns to the future.)*

5. Examine the importance and effectiveness of the narrator who begins and ends the story. *(The narrator gives important information about the Traveller that is not revealed in the chapters narrated by the Traveller. He sets the stage for the Traveller's departure and tells about his condition when he returns. In the closing section, he reveals the response of others to the Traveller's story, he tells about the Traveller's second departure, and he reflects on the state of humanity.)*

6. Discuss what motivates the Time Traveller to travel into the future rather than into the past. Would you travel into the future or the past if you could travel in time? *(Answers will vary.)*

7. Analyze what the Time Traveller discovers about future society. Discuss possible positive or negative effects on people of the future if future generations eliminate poverty, successfully clone humans, eliminate disease, eliminate pollution, find the "fountain of youth," etc. *(Information about the future society is presented throughout this guide.)*

8. Examine how Wells presents his own belief system in the novel, e.g., the division of social classes, his concerns about the future of humanity, the importance of human intellect, the dangers of capitalism and industrialization. *(Wells criticized the aristocracy, yet the Traveller sympathizes with the Eloi [former aristocracy] rather than the Morlocks [working class]. The Eloi have lost their intellectual ability because they ceased to use it, reflecting Wells' concern that people can grow too self-centered when searching only for pleasure. The book foreshadows the decline of humanity and the ultimate end of the earth as Wells' generation knew it. The Morlocks' superiority reflects his concern about the effects of the industrial revolution on humans, i.e., that machines would become more important than people.)*

9. Examine why Weena is the only one of the future people who is named and examine the relationship between her and the Traveller. *(Answers will vary. Their relationship is addressed in the Discussion Questions.)*

10. Analyze the significance of the title of the novel. *(In the novel, the Traveller journeys into the future via the Time Machine and could as easily have journeyed into the past. Wells uses the Traveller's journey into the future to give his predictions about future society and to warn against the dangers of society's division into social stratifications. Note also that the novel itself, written in 1895, has lasted over a century and remains a timeless classic.)*

11. Utilize the definition for utopia to discuss why the Traveller changes his mind about having found a future social paradise and whether or not it is possible to find a utopia. *(Utopia: ideal society with justice and equality for all citizens. Answers will vary.)*

12. Analyze the symbolism of the White Sphinx, the Palace of Green Porcelain, the white flowers, and the sunset. *(Answers are found in the Discussion Questions.)*

Post-reading Extension Activities

Note: Starred items indicate enrichment for accelerated students.

Writing
1. Write name poems for two of the Time Traveller's guests at one of his dinners.
2. *Write a sequel to the novel after the Traveller returns again.
3. Write a diamente poem contrasting the Eloi and the Morlocks.
4. Write a title for each chapter.

Art
1. Create a collage depicting the light and dark emotions of the book.
2. Prepare a poster to advertise the book.
3. *Prepare a series of sketches that tell the Traveller's story.

Viewing
1. View the movie version of *The Time Machine* and present an oral comparison of the movie with the novel.

Music
1. *Write and perform a ballad that tells the story of the Time Traveller and Weena.
2. Play for the class one or two musical selections that appropriately fit the book's content.

Current Events
1. *Bring to class newspaper or magazine articles that predict the future. These may relate to ecology, scientific experiments, global warming, etc. Choose one article and write a brief narrative set in a future world where this prediction has come true.

Media
1. Write a newspaper article about the Traveller's return from the Journalist's point of view.
2. *Write and stage a press conference with the narrator in the Traveller's laboratory after his second departure. This can be presented via a video presentation or staged before the class.

Assessment for *The Time Machine*

Assessment is an ongoing process. The following ten items can be completed during the novel study. Once finished, the student and teacher will check the work. Points may be added to indicate the level of understanding.

Name _____ Date _____

Student   **Teacher**

_____   _____   1. Correct any quizzes taken over the novel.

_____   _____   2. Write two review questions over the novel and use these to participate in an oral review.

_____   _____   3. Display or perform your extension projects on an assigned day. Be prepared to explain your projects.

_____   _____   4. Working in a small group, present one of the scenes from the novel in a charade and have the class guess the scene you are portraying.

_____   _____   5. Participate in a vocabulary "bee." You are to supply the definition of each word rather than the spelling.

_____   _____   6. Compare any activities, such as Character Webs and Story Maps, in small groups of three or four.

_____   _____   7. Write two questions you would like to ask the Time Traveller. Exchange with a partner and answer his or her questions as if you were the Time Traveller.

_____   _____   8. Write a review of the book for the school newspaper. Use at least ten of your vocabulary words from the novel.

_____   _____   9. Write the name of the character the teacher is describing as s/he gives descriptive words of the book's characters.

_____   _____   10. Write a metaphor or a simile from your list on a slip of paper. Exchange with a partner and identify each other's literary device.

Linking Novel Units® Tests to National and State Reading Assessments

During the past several years, an increasing number of students have faced some form of state-mandated competency testing in reading. Many states now administer reading assessments to measure the skills and knowledge emphasized in their particular reading curriculum. The Discussion Questions and Post-reading Discussion Questions in this Novel Units® Teacher Guide make excellent open-ended comprehension questions that may be used throughout the daily lessons as practice activities. The rubric below provides important information for evaluating responses to open-ended comprehension questions. Teachers may also use scoring rubrics provided for their own state's competency test. *Plese note*: The Novel Units® Student Packet contains optional open-ended questions in a format similar to many national and state rading assessments.

Scoring Rubric for Open-Ended Items

3-Exemplary	Thorough, complete ideas/information Clear organization throughout Logical reasoning/conclusions Thorough understanding of reading task Accurate, complete response
2-Sufficient	Many relevant ideas/pieces of information Clear organization throughout most of response Minor problems in logical reasoning/conclusions General understanding of reading task Generally accurate and complete response
1-Partially Sufficient	Minimally relevant ideas/information Obvious gaps in organization Obvious problems in logical reasoning/conclusions Minimal understanding of reading task Inaccuracies/incomplete response
0-Insufficient	Irrelevant ideas/information No coherent organization Major problems in logical reasoning/conclusions Little or no understanding of reading task Generally inaccurate/incomplete response

Glossary

Chapter 1, pp. 3–11
1. recondite (3): hard to understand; profound
2. paradox (4): a statement that may be true but seems to say two contradictory things
3. fecundity (4): fertility; fruitfulness; abundant productivity
4. introspective (5): meditative; inclined to examine one's own thoughts and feelings
5. communistic (8): supporting the political and economic system in which the government owns the land, factories, and other economic resources
6. plausible (11): appearing true or reasonable

Chapter 2, pp. 12–17
1. ingenuity (12): resourcefulness; inventiveness
2. anachronism (12): something or someone that is not in its correct historical or chronological time
3. jocular (13): facetious; witty; given to joking
4. cadger (14): traveling peddler; lowly worker, similar to a tramp
5. caricature (15): exaggeration; an imitation or copy so distorted or inferior as to be ludicrous
6. verbatim (16): word-for-word
7. intonation (17): expression; rise and fall in tone of voice

Chapter 3, pp. 17–22
1. velocity (18): rate of speed at which something happens
2. luminous (18): radiating or reflecting light
3. rudimentary (19): undeveloped; fundamental; primary
4. sphinx (21): statue of a mythological creature having the body of a lion and the head of a human; some had an eagle's wings and a serpent's tail
5. verdigris (21): green coating that forms like rust on certain metals
6. temerity (21): foolhardiness; reckless boldness
7. consumptive (22): person afflicted with tuberculosis, which was once known as consumption; tubercular

Chapter 4, pp. 22–32
1. hypertrophied (25): overgrown; abnormally enlarged
2. indolent (26): lazy; idle; disliking work
3. precipitous (27): extremely steep
4. intimation (27): hint; suggestion
5. precocious (28): unusually advanced or mature in knowledge or skills
6. griffins (29): fabled monsters, usually having the head and wings of an eagle and the body of a lion
7. ameliorating (29): making or becoming better; improving
8. subjugation (30): under complete control of another
9. connubial (31): of marriage

Chapter 5, pp. 32–48
1. inarticulate (34): lacking the ability to express oneself in clear or effective speech
2. stolid (36): unemotional; impassive
3. repugnance (36): strong distaste, aversion, or loathing
4. monomania (37): mental disorder in which a person is obsessed or controlled by a single idea or emotion
5. subterranean (38): under the surface of the earth
6. decadent (39): declining culturally or morally; decaying
7. interpolated (40): interjected; altered by inserting something new
8. expostulations (41): protests; objections
9. lemur (44): furry, nocturnal animal; resembles a monkey but with a longer, sharper nose
10. nocturnal (45): active at night
11. ramifications (46): results; offshoots, i.e., underground caverns spreading everywhere

Chapter 6, pp. 48–53
1. pallid (48): lacking color; pale
2. façade (49): front part of a building
3. disconcerted (50): confused; embarrassed
4. abysmal (51): having immense or fathomless extension downward
5. carnivorous (51): using other animals as food; man-eating
6. lank (52): long and thin; slender

Chapter 7, pp. 54–60
1. malign (54): injurious; malicious; hateful
2. hypothesis (54): tentative assumption; guess
3. evolution (55): process of formation or growth; gradual development
4. Nemesis (55): destiny; doom
5. dexterous (56): quick and skillful in bodily movements
6. preternaturally (56): abnormally; mysteriously; supernaturally
7. vigil (58): act of keeping awake during the usual hours of sleep for some purpose; watchfulness
8. degradation (59): humiliation; degeneration

Chapter 8, pp. 60–66
1. vestiges (60): remnants; all that remains
2. oblique (61): slanting; non-horizontal
3. deliquesced (62): melted or became liquid by absorbing moisture from the air
4. derelict (64): abandoned, forsaken, deserted
5. hermetically (65): tightly closed so that air cannot get out
6. volatile (65): explosive; evaporating quickly

Chapters 9–10, pp. 66–75
1. insidious (67): crafty; tricky; treacherous
2. carbuncles (69): precious gems that are smooth, round, and deep red
3. agape (70): with the mouth wide open in wonder and surprise
4. abominations (72): things that arouse strong disgust or loathing; revolting things

Chapter 11, pp. 76–80
1. prodigious (76): huge; vast; amazing
2. sullen (77): irritable; gloomy or dismal
3. lurid (77): lighted up with red or fiery glare
4. apparition (78): supernatural sight or thing
5. foliated (78): having leaves
6. undulating (79): having a wavy motion; surging

Chapter 12–Epilogue, pp. 81–86
1. stagnant (82): not active; sluggish or dull
2. translucent (84): letting light through; transparent
3. truncated (85): cut off
4. phantasm (85): supposed appearance of an absent person; ghost
5. abysses (86): bottomless pits; lowest depths